BOLD
COMPOSER

A Creative Minds Biography

BOLD COMPOSER

A Story about Ludwig van Beethoven

by Judith P. Josephson

illustrations by Barbara Kiwak

M Millbrook Press/Minneapolis

For my parents, who gave me the gift of music
— J. P. J.

My thanks to Edith Fine, Karen Coombs, Donna Agins, and my critique group. Thanks also to Dan Swem, Patricia Stroh, and the Ira F. Brilliant Beethoven Museum at San Jose State University, and my editor, Susan Rose

Milbrook Press, Inc.
A division of Lerner Publishing Group
241 First Avenue North
Minneapolis, MN 55401 U.S.A.

Website address: www.lernerbooks.com

Library of Congress Cataloging-in-Publication Data

Josephson, Judith Pinkerton.
    Bold Composer: a story about Ludwig van Beethoven / by Judith P.
  Josephson ; illustrations by Barbara Kiwak.
      p.   cm. — (A creative minds biography)
    Includes bibliographical references and index.
    ISBN-13: 978–0–8225–5987–0 (lib. bdg. : alk. paper)
    ISBN-10: 0–8225–5987–0 (lib. bdg. : alk. paper)
    1. Beethoven, Ludwig van, 1770–1827—Juvenile literature.
  2. Composers—Austria—Biography—Juvenile literature. I. Kiwak,
  Barbara, ill. II. Title. III. Series.
  ML3930.B4J67 2007
  780.92—dc22   2006000703

Manufactured in the United States of America
1 2 3 4 5 6 – JR – 12 11 10 09 08 07

Table of Contents

1

Music, Always Music

Young Ludwig van Beethoven ducked into a hen-house. Smells of musty hay and chickens filled his nose. Sunlight peeked through the wood slats, making striped patterns on the floor. Creeping toward the nests, Ludwig sneaked his hand under one hen's warm feathers.

He heard his neighbor Frau Fischer bustling across the courtyard. She scolded him for stealing her eggs but smiled, calling him an egg fox.

"I am more of a music fox . . . than an egg fox," said Ludwig.

Ludwig loved music. He heard music in the squeak of the iron window handles. Starting at the age of three or four, he plunked out melodies on the clavichord, an early keyboard instrument.

Ludwig van Beethoven was born on December 16, 1770, in the small town of Bonn in the German part of the Holy Roman Empire. For hundreds of years, the Holy Roman Empire had controlled many governments throughout Europe. Bonn's dusty, tree-lined streets wound past old houses with gardens, a market square, and town hall. Chickens and pigs roamed freely.

Ludwig's father, Johann, played the violin, sang, and taught music. Musicians usually worked for wealthy people, the royal family, or church leaders, but they weren't paid well. So the Beethovens never had much money. Ludwig wore shabby clothes. His dark hair stuck out in matted clumps.

"Why do you look dirty?" Frau Fischer once asked. "You should make yourself proper."

"When I grow up, nobody will worry about it," Ludwig said.

His father taught him how to read musical notes and to play using both hands. Ludwig quickly understood how musical notes fit together in rhythms and patterns.

Johann van Beethoven thought there was only one right way to learn an instrument—step-by-step. He was a strict teacher. He slapped Ludwig's hands if he didn't play the right notes. Standing on a little bench to play, Ludwig sometimes cried as he practiced.

Ludwig's mother, Maria Magdalena, wasn't sure how to raise her bright, unusual eldest child. Caring for her younger children left little time for Ludwig. Carl was born in 1774, and Johann in 1776. Four other babies died in infancy. Though Ludwig's mother was loving, he often felt lonely and neglected.

His demanding father rarely praised the boy. Yet Johann bragged to others, "My son Ludwig is my only joy. . . . I know that some day he'll be a great man of the world."

Sometimes Ludwig propped his elbows on the windowsill, chin in his hands, and daydreamed. One day Frau Fischer called to him, "How are you, Ludwig?" No answer. She tried again. The boy still didn't answer. Then she said, "Foul weather seems to be with you."

"Please, no, no! Forgive me!" he said. "I was busy with such a beautiful, deep thought I couldn't bear to be disturbed."

A short boy with bright, merry eyes, Ludwig liked to ride piggyback with his friends. They played at the palace where his father and grandfather worked. Bonn's musical life centered on the royal court and the palace. Ludwig's grandfather, a fine singer and keyboard player, held the important job of *kapellmeister*—director of the choir and orchestra. He took charge of all the music for dances, banquets, plays, and church services.

Other Bonn musicians often gathered at the Beethoven home. The visitors and the Beethovens played instruments, sang, and talked about music.

Ludwig's every moment seemed filled with music. Music for breakfast, music for dinner—music, always music.

Johann hoped his son would become another Wolfgang Amadeus Mozart. Born fourteen years before Ludwig, young Mozart had shown amazing talent as a performer and as a composer, writing musical works. In concerts throughout Europe, Mozart had earned money for his family. Ludwig's father hoped his son would do the same. By the age of seven, Ludwig played the keyboard well enough to perform a few pieces at a concert in nearby Cologne.

Ludwig attended school, where he studied writing, reading, and arithmetic. At first, his handwriting was neat and careful. Gradually, it became messier. Subjects such as spelling and punctuation puzzled Ludwig. He could add simple numbers but could not multiply.

Like music, languages came easily to him. Ludwig spoke his native German and some French, and he read Latin and Italian. Music for singers was often written in Italian. Directions written on music, such as *pianissimo* for very quiet and *forte* for loud, were also in Italian.

During his school years, Ludwig's restless father often moved his family from one apartment to another. This was hard on the Beethovens. Ludwig's formal schooling ended when he was eleven, which was common at the time. Ludwig continued to read about many subjects on his own.

He began studying music with thirty-three-year-old Christian Gottlob Neefe. A gentle, well-read man, Neefe was a respected musician, composer, and teacher. He played the organ, directed a local theater group, and was choir director at Bonn's chapel. He sensed Ludwig's fierce concentration.

Under Neefe's guidance, Ludwig's talent blossomed. Ludwig learned about religious music—

music played for church services. He learned about theatrical music—music for the theater. He learned to play the violin and viola. And he learned about orchestral music—music for a large group of string, wind, brass, and percussion instruments.

Ludwig studied great composers, such as Johann Sebastian Bach, who had died in 1750. Bach's music required a new way of playing—curving the hands and using all the fingers. Ludwig was good at this. "If you are able to play Bach well, you can play practically any composer," Neefe told his young student. The music of twenty-five-year-old Mozart also thrilled Ludwig.

He began to write his own music. Neefe explained how to show emotion by changing the music from slow to fast, from soft to loud.

In 1782, when he was eleven, Ludwig's first keyboard work was published. It was nine variations, or versions, of a popular march.

After a year, Neefe asked Ludwig to help with some of his duties. Ludwig accompanied orchestra rehearsals. He played the organ at Mass, a church service, early in the morning. Before dawn, Ludwig hurried through the dark streets of Bonn. Short and hunched over, he drew his wool coat around him as he walked. At the chapel, candles on the walls and atop the small organ cast a warm glow on people sitting in the shadowy pews.

Ludwig climbed up on the seat of the organ. In front of him, three keyboards stair-stepped, one above the other. Twelve-year-old Ludwig stretched his arms and curved his fingers above the keys. Then he began to play. Rippling notes echoed off the stone walls as music greeted the dawn.

2

A Guiding Spirit

Ludwig believed he had an inner spirit who guided him, his unseen Muse. "Write down for once the harmonies of your soul!" his Muse often whispered to him. So whenever Ludwig had a musical idea, he scribbled it down.

He carefully studied the music of other composers. Then he wrote music his own way. In 1783 three of Ludwig's keyboard pieces, Sonatas for Clavier, were published. Written for one or two instruments, a sonata had three or four parts. *Clavier* was a general term for keyboard instruments, such as the clavichord, the harpsichord, and the piano (sometimes called a pianoforte). Invented in the early 1700s, the piano was just becoming popular with musicians and composers. For the first time, keyboard players could play louder by pressing harder on the keys and play more softly by pressing more gently.

In a music magazine, Ludwig's teacher described how well his pupil played especially difficult pieces, such as *The Well-Tempered Clavier* by Johann Sebastian Bach. Neefe called Ludwig a young genius and said he could become another Mozart.

Near the end of 1783, Ludwig and his mother visited a cousin in Holland. On their wintry boat journey up the Rhine River, Ludwig's mother held her son's feet in her lap so they wouldn't freeze. In Holland, Ludwig gave concerts in mansions and at the Dutch government center. Ludwig's confidence and skill amazed people. But Ludwig didn't think people paid him enough. "The Dutch are penny-pinchers!" he said. "I'll never go to Holland again."

In 1784 Christian Neefe became Bonn's court organist and Ludwig became his paid assistant. Ludwig learned to play major works by the composers Wolfgang Amadeus Mozart, George Frideric Handel, and Franz Joseph Haydn. By the age of fourteen, Ludwig also played viola at court or church as a member of an orchestra. The viola was larger than a violin with deeper tones.

Ludwig also played for operas—musical plays with singing, drama, and scenery. One of the newest operas was Mozart's *The Marriage of Figaro*. One day, Ludwig hoped to write his own opera.

For fancy occasions or concerts, Ludwig wore his royal court uniform. It was a sea green coat, embroidered vest, knee-length trousers with buckles, silk stockings, and shoes with chunky heels. Instead of letting his hair fly around, he tied it back neatly at the neck, curling the sides in the fashion of the day.

Even when dressed up, Ludwig didn't consider himself attractive. Only five feet four inches tall, he was stocky with broad shoulders and a short neck. His head was large with a broad forehead, a big nose, and small, expressive brown eyes. Like many other people in Europe, he'd had smallpox. The disease had scarred his face.

During this time, Ludwig struck up a friendship with a young medical student, Franz Wegeler. Wegeler introduced Ludwig to the von Breunings, a well-to-do, cultured family. In the many days and nights he spent at their home, Ludwig learned about German literature, especially the plays and poetry of Johann Wolfgang von Goethe. The famous Goethe was one of the most beloved German writers. An idea came to Ludwig—to write music for Goethe's poems.

In April 1787, sixteen-year-old Beethoven traveled to Vienna, a city high above the Danube River. Surrounded by fields of cornflowers and poppies as well as deep, dark woods, it was twenty times larger than Bonn. Tall buildings, glittering palaces, and busy shops lined Vienna's broad streets.

In Vienna, Beethoven hoped to study with Wolfgang Amadeus Mozart. When Beethoven played a keyboard piece for the thirty-year-old Mozart, Mozart seemed unimpressed. That didn't stop Beethoven. He convinced the music master to name a melody. Then Ludwig instantly made up a variation on the melody. Mozart listened, amazed at the inventiveness of Beethoven's playing.

Later, Mozart told his friends: "Keep your eyes on him. Someday he will give the world something to talk about."

Ludwig had been in Vienna only a few weeks when an urgent letter arrived. Come home quickly, his father wrote. Ludwig's mother was dying. The five-hundred-mile journey by horse and carriage took several days. Back in Bonn, he found his mother weak from tuberculosis, a serious lung disease. She died a few months later, on July 17, 1787, at the age of forty.

Heartsick with grief, Ludwig said his mother had been his best friend. "She was such a kind, loving mother to me," he wrote. His brother Carl was thirteen, and Johann was eleven.

After his wife's death, Ludwig's father spent more and more money on alcohol. When he drank, he became angry and violent. When sober, he was brooding and unhappy. Sometimes Ludwig pleaded with police not to put his father in jail for his loud, rowdy behavior. Just two months after his mother died, Ludwig's baby sister, Maria Margaretha, also died.

Ludwig became the head of the Beethoven family. His music earned money, but not enough to care for the whole family. Sometimes Ludwig's chest felt tight and he couldn't breathe. He worried that he would die of lung disease like his mother.

Friends helped. Helene von Breuning nursed Ludwig through his frequent illnesses and dark moods. Her son Stephan and Ludwig became closer friends.

All the while, Ludwig's skills as a pianist and composer grew. An older friend, Count Ferdinand Waldstein, saw Ludwig's enormous talent. He gave Ludwig money so he had time to practice and write music.

On February 20, 1790, Emperor Joseph II died in Vienna. Ludwig, nineteen, was chosen to compose music to honor the emperor. Ludwig's songlike *Cantata on the Death of Emperor Joseph II* called for many instruments. Some musicians said it was too hard to play, so it wasn't performed at the time.

On December 5, 1791, Wolfgang Amadeus Mozart died at the age of thirty-five. This ended Beethoven's dream of studying with the famous composer.

But Beethoven had also met the sixty-year-old composer Franz Joseph Haydn, Europe's most famous musical figure and a huge admirer of Mozart. Haydn promised to teach Ludwig if he moved to Vienna. Beethoven decided to go. His friend Count Waldstein said that he was going to "receive the spirit of Mozart from Haydn's hands."

3

On to Vienna

Early on the morning of November 2, 1792, twenty-one-year-old Ludwig left Bonn by horse-drawn carriage to move to Vienna. In his trunk were musical sketches and a few personal belongings. Along the way, he jotted down his thoughts in a small diary.

Vienna buzzed like a beehive with music making. Of the 200,000 people who lived there, 6,000 were pianists. Rich people wanted good music played in their elegant homes. And musicians needed the help of such supporters. But in Vienna, musicians, jugglers, acrobats, and puppeteers also performed on the streets for poor people.

Ludwig soon made a list of things he needed—firewood, coffee, overcoat, boots, shoes, a piano, and a writing desk. He also decided he needed a dancing teacher. People often danced at parties, and Beethoven was clumsy and awkward.

Vienna was known for its fine food. Ludwig's tastes were simple. Favorite meals included macaroni with Parmesan cheese, bland stews, mushy bread soup made with ten fresh eggs, and fish. He drank strong coffee, sixty coffee beans per cup, and spring water.

Once he invited some new friends over. He greeted them dressed in a short evening jacket, a blue apron over his pants, and a nightcap on top of his unruly hair. He served undercooked beef and vegetables floating in water and grease. His guests decided Ludwig wasn't much of a cook.

A month after he arrived in Vienna, a letter came from his brother Johann. Their father had died on December 18, 1792. Ludwig didn't return to Bonn for the funeral. He didn't even mention his father's death in his diary.

For a short time, Ludwig, twenty-two, moved to a mansion owned by Prince Karl Lichnowsky. The prince treated Beethoven like an honored guest and friend. Prince Karl told his servants to answer whenever Beethoven rang the bell in his room.

In spite of such generosity, Beethoven fussed when asked to appear each afternoon for the day's main meal. How ridiculous, he thought, to have to go home, change his clothes, and shave!

For six months, Beethoven studied with Franz Joseph Haydn. Beethoven looked up to Haydn, but the two were very different. Haydn was a gentleman with fine manners. Beethoven had a hot temper and bad manners. The two composers also wrote music very differently. Haydn's music followed orderly patterns in the classical style of the day. Beethoven kept trying out new ways to play the piano and write music. When Haydn criticized him, Beethoven felt hurt. Still, the patient, older musician tried to teach his fiery young student how to make his musical ideas stronger.

Beethoven studied violin and piano with other teachers too, but he told them not to tell Haydn. Beethoven also worked on his conducting. To get musicians to play louder, he'd leap up and fling his arms wildly or thwack his baton against the stand. To make musicians play softer, he'd crouch down low. Orchestras often had trouble following him. But when he liked what they did, he'd smile and shout, *"Bravi tutti!"* meaning "Very good, all!"

Ludwig's favorite composers were Mozart, Bach,

and Handel. Beethoven admired how Handel had taken simple melodies and, from them, created wonderful music.

Ludwig wrote often to his brothers and friends in Bonn. In one 1793 letter, he thanked Christian Gottlob Neefe for all he'd taught him.

Counts and countesses—members of the royal court—invited Beethoven to play piano in their homes. Though he needed their support and interest, he sometimes said no. When he did play, he didn't always follow the notes written on the page. Instead, he improvised, making up melodies as he played. Sometimes other pianists took turns improvising with Beethoven, turning the concert into a contest. The audience decided who had been most creative. (Beethoven usually won.)

Many musicians wore powdered wigs and elegant clothes. But Beethoven wore his hair loose and bristly around his face. His clothes were often rumpled. He spoke plainly and didn't bother to be polite. Sometimes before a concert, he peered out at the audience to make sure no one he disliked was there.

But once Beethoven's broad-tipped fingers pounded over the keys, most people forgave him for his rudeness. His brilliant playing made some people weep with joy.

Eventually Ludwig earned enough money to help his brothers move to Vienna. Carl taught music for a while. Then he took a job as a clerk in a bank. Johann became a pharmacist.

In 1796, when Ludwig was twenty-five, he performed in other important European musical centers—Berlin, Dresden, Leipzig, and Prague. In Prague, Ludwig wrote to his brother Johann, "I am well, very well. My art is winning me friends and fame, and what more do I want? And this time I will make a good deal of money." He kept careful track of his expenses, even writing down if he spent a penny for coffee.

For everything Beethoven composed, publishers competed to publish and sell his music. Publishing took a long time. Engravers etched the music onto copper plates and hand-punched the words onto elegant manuscripts. This left room for mistakes, something Beethoven hated: "Mistakes—mistakes—you yourself are a unique mistake!" he told one publisher. "I will have to send my copyist, or go there myself, if I want to ensure that my works don't come out as just a mass of mistakes."

Unlike most musicians, Beethoven was earning enough money to support himself. He could now afford to live comfortably. Restless, he moved from apartment to apartment, carting his instruments and secondhand furniture with him. Sometimes Ludwig rented two or three apartments at once. He spent summers in the country. There, as he rambled through rolling hills, flowers, and deep woods, his musical ideas flowed. "No one can love the country as much as I do," he said.

In his diary, Beethoven wrote about his frequent headaches, bronchitis, and stomach problems. But his will to succeed was strong. One of his New Year's resolutions read, "Courage. Even with all the frailties of my body, my spirit shall rule."

4

A Great Silence

When Beethoven was about twenty-eight, he started hearing noises that no one else could hear. Some sounds screeched like crickets inside his ears. Others echoed like foghorns or rang like gongs. These maddening sounds frightened him.

Beethoven's hearing was his most important sense. He even had the ability to hear and remember notes in his head. (Some people called this having perfect pitch.) Music was his life!

At first, he blamed the noises on his poor health. He thought the sounds would go away. Instead, they grew worse. At concerts he couldn't hear the higher notes. If people spoke softly or turned away, he missed what they said.

Doctors ordered strengthening medicines, herbs, and almond oil—common remedies of the day. Beethoven took cold baths and swam in the Danube River. Nothing worked, but he continued to enjoy his baths, especially pouring water over his head.

On June 29, 1801, Beethoven, thirty, wrote to his childhood friend Franz Wegeler, by this time a medical doctor: "My ears continue to hum and buzz day and night. . . . I lead a miserable life."

Although shy, Beethoven took pleasure in talking to people. But because of his hearing problems, he stopped going to parties. He structured his days in a regular pattern. Starting at dawn, he worked until the afternoon, taking breaks for walks. Sometimes he stopped into cafés and read newspapers. At night he'd play the violin, viola, or piano. By ten o'clock, he was in bed. "I live entirely in my music; and hardly have I completed one composition [musical work] than I have already begun another," he wrote. "At my present rate of composing, I often produce three or four works at a time."

In the past, he had written rough drafts on loose sheets of paper. Now he organized his music in bound sketchbooks. Whenever he went out, he carried small notebooks for jotting down ideas. Later, he recorded them in his sketchbooks.

From 1798 to 1802, Ludwig filled seven sketchbooks. He wrote music for solo piano and violin, as well as for larger groups. He wrote a ballet for dancers and orchestra. His first two symphonies, large works for many different instruments, contained several sections, or movements. Beethoven revised his works again and again. By saving every draft, he kept track of changes he made. Even after works were published, he kept his notebooks and papers, stashing them in messy piles.

Carl Beethoven became Ludwig's business manager. His brother made sure concert organizers and publishers paid Ludwig well.

Sounds in Ludwig's world slowly became more muffled. He told his violinist friend Karl Amenda, "I am cut off from everything dear and precious to me." Yet he asked Amenda to keep his growing hearing loss a secret.

Then Ludwig fell in love with his seventeen-year-old piano student, Countess Giulietta Guicciardi. He called her a "dear enchanting girl who loves me and whom I love." In her honor, he wrote a beautiful piano piece, the *Moonlight* Sonata. But their love didn't last. A few years later, Giulietta married someone else.

Beethoven threw himself into performing, conducting, and composing. In his string quartets—written for two violins, a viola, and a cello—players answered one another's melodies. This created a musical conversation.

Doctors suggested that Beethoven rest his ears and spend time in the countryside. Beginning in April

1802, he spent six months in the village of Heiligenstadt near Vienna. Here he'd have more time to compose.

Immediately, he wrote two sets of variations and three sonatas for piano. "Usually I have to wait for other people to tell me when I have new ideas, because I never know this myself," he told his publisher. But this time, Beethoven knew his ideas were fresh and new.

Beethoven, thirty-one, relaxed in the peacefulness of Heiligenstadt. But his health problems threatened something he loved as much as living—hearing music. Beethoven believed his hearing should be more perfect than anyone else's.

On October 6, 1802, he wrote a private letter in the form of a will for his two brothers. Admitting that he had a fiery temper, he tried to explain his changeable moods. He also explained how embarrassed he felt about his hearing: "It was impossible for me to say to people, 'speak louder, shout, for I am deaf.' How humiliated I have felt if somebody standing beside me heard the sound of a flute in the distance and I heard nothing."

He wrote to his brothers that if he died, they should divide his money fairly and be kind to each other. He told them that qualities like goodness and virtue, not money, had helped him in his darkest moments. "Perhaps my condition will improve; perhaps not," he added. He said he didn't fear death but asked God to give him one day of pure happiness.

Beethoven hoped his health would improve. But even if it didn't, he had reached a turning point. He no longer thought about death. Instead, he chose to live and create music.

5

A New Way

Beethoven returned to Vienna on October 10, 1802. He put his will away among his private papers. Filled with new energy, he said he didn't think he had written his best music yet. He wanted to give the world all the music he still had within him. "From this day on I shall take a new way."

He began an oratorio, a religious work for singers and orchestra. Called *Christ on the Mount of Olives*, it told the story of Jesus' suffering before he was crucified. The words and music expressed loneliness, fear, and anger but also love and triumph.

Early in 1803, Beethoven, thirty-two, became a resident composer at the Theater an der Wien, Vienna's main theater. Beethoven and his brother moved into rooms there. Carl helped arrange a grand concert for April 5, 1803. It would include Beethoven's first two symphonies, the oratorio, and a piano concerto—a piece for solo instrument and orchestra.

At five o'clock in the morning on the day of the concert, Beethoven was still writing a trombone part for the oratorio. At eight o'clock, he and the musicians began rehearsing. After six hours, they stopped for lunch. Then they rehearsed some more.

That night, Beethoven's friend Ignaz von Seyfried was to turn pages during the piano concerto. Beethoven began to play. His friend saw not music but squiggles and strange marks on the paper. Beethoven hadn't had time to write down the piano notes! Luckily, Beethoven signaled Ignaz when he wanted him to turn the page.

After the concert, the two friends laughed about the pages without notes. Beethoven's laugh sounded liked a lion roaring.

By tripling ticket prices for this concert, Beethoven earned more than he usually did in one year. His fans willingly paid extra to see him play and to listen to his powerful music.

During this time, he began an opera. First titled *Leonore*, then *Fidelio*, the opera was about freedom and married love. The heroine dressed as a man in order to rescue her innocent husband from jail. This make-believe character was Beethoven's ideal woman—devoted and loving.

In February 1804, the Theater an der Wien was sold to a new owner. Beethoven lost his job, as well as his place to live. He called his new lodgings "a wretched hole." Soon he moved again to share an apartment with his old friend Stephan von Breuning.

In the fall of 1804, Beethoven, thirty-three, began giving piano lessons to a lovely countess named Josephine Deym, twenty-six. Beethoven was a friend of her family. Josephine's husband had recently died, leaving her with four young children. Beethoven wrote thirteen love letters to her, calling her his "only beloved." He signed one, "Your Beethoven, Who Worships You."

When Ludwig asked Josephine to marry him, she said no. If she married him, she would no longer be a countess. Even more important, marriage laws of those times would not allow her to raise her four children herself. More letters passed between them, but nothing came of their love.

Beethoven continued to work on *Leonore*. He

also worked on his Third Symphony. From its beginning notes, it differed greatly from other symphonies of that time. Beethoven passed the melody from one instrument to the next. He wrote sudden changes in mood, rhythm, and key. The symphony was also longer than his first two symphonies. One critic said Beethoven might start a musical revolution. In fact, his music was changing from the more traditional classical style of Haydn and Mozart to an entirely new emotional and dramatic style.

Not everyone liked Beethoven's music. Some people said it was too jolting, even shocking. Some parts were soft and sad, others suddenly loud and angry, still others lilting and joyful. Beethoven used simple melodies that kept repeating and building into a mass of deep, rich sound. Sometimes the music appeared to be ending with strong, final-sounding notes. Then— surprise!—it continued.

Audiences had to pay attention to understand his music. Some people just wanted to flutter their fans, sip wine, or chat as they listened to music in the background. But if people talked, Beethoven would stop playing and stalk away.

To those who said his music was too hard to understand or play, Beethoven said, "Don't worry. This is music for a later age."

He dedicated his Third Symphony to Napoleon Bonaparte, the leader of France. Beethoven thought Napoleon believed in rights for poor people and freedom for all. But in December 1804, Napoleon crowned himself emperor, the all-powerful ruler of France.

When Beethoven heard the news, he crossed out Napoleon's name on the title page of his symphony, tore it in half, and threw it on the floor. Napoleon would become a tyrant, he shouted!

Beethoven's temper flared at other times. He hired and fired maids, cooks, and other servants. Often he accused them of stealing, misplacing his things, or reading his mail. During a rehearsal, if he didn't like the way an instrument sounded, he threw himself on the floor in a rage.

Sometimes suspicious and distrustful of his friends, he got mad at them too. One night during dinner with Stephan von Breuning, the two friends argued. Beethoven jumped up, knocked over a chair, and yelled. Later, he asked his friend to forgive him.

Despite Beethoven's stormy moods, most of his friends found him honest, generous, and fun loving. He enjoyed puns, pranks, and jokes. At times, Beethoven startled audiences by standing up after a concert and bellowing with laughter.

But when he was working, Beethoven hated to be disturbed. He also forgot about practical things, such as eating or giving piano lessons. One of his piano students was Ferdinand Ries, a friend and composer. One day before his lesson, Ries joined Beethoven on a long walk. The whole time, Beethoven hummed and wailed up and down the scale. He clasped his hands behind his back. His hair was wild under his top hat. When Ries asked what he was singing, Beethoven said he'd had an idea for the last movement of his new piano sonata.

Once home, Beethoven rushed to the piano without taking off his hat. Ries sat down to listen. Beethoven's hairy hands moved nimbly along the keyboard. The muscles of his face tightened. His mouth trembled.

Much later, Beethoven looked up, surprised to see Ries. "I cannot give you a lesson today," Beethoven said. "I still have work to do." Then he continued, trying out new combinations of notes.

6

The Art of Music

Beethoven's Third Symphony was first performed on April 7, 1805. Some people loved this symphony, called *Eroica*—meaning "the story of a hero." Others thought it was too heavy and long.

That fall, Napoleon's French troops occupied Vienna. Exploding shells boomed. On the streets, people fought for food.

At the theater, musicians and singers rehearsed Beethoven's opera, now called *Fidelio*. After a five-week delay, the opera opened. Most of Beethoven's friends and fans had fled Vienna, so the audience was mostly French officers. They didn't like it. The opera soon closed.

Supporters and friends urged Beethoven to shorten the opera. At first, he refused. Finally, he agreed.

A few days later, the tenor soloist stopped by to pick up his revised solo. He found Beethoven sitting in a huge tub, laughing loudly as he poured buckets of water over himself. He rose from the tub and toweled dry, talking about the revisions. When the reworked opera was performed that spring, audiences liked it better.

On May 25, 1806, Ludwig's brother Carl married Johanna Reiss. A few months later, Johanna gave birth to Karl Beethoven. From time to time, Ludwig helped his brother Carl by giving him money.

To Beethoven's great relief, Napoleon and his troops left Vienna to fight elsewhere. Life in Vienna returned to normal. By the summer of 1808, Beethoven, thirty-seven, had finished his Fourth, Fifth, and Sixth Symphonies. Beethoven had been thinking about leaving Vienna to become a court composer in Kassel. Vienna's royalty and leaders didn't want such a talented musician and composer to leave their city. Two princes and an archduke convinced Beethoven to stay in Vienna by offering to pay him a yearly salary. Beethoven's music continued to grow and change.

When people first heard Beethoven's mighty Fifth Symphony, they called it powerful, astonishing, wild. Audiences loved the energy of the first four notes—DA, DA, DA, DUM!—three short notes all the same, then one long, lower note. To respond to their enthusiasm, Beethoven often ended concerts with the Fifth Symphony.

Beethoven's Sixth Symphony, called the *Pastoral* Symphony, showed his love for nature and the countryside. In its slow movement, listeners could almost hear birds chirping and see sheep grazing alongside a bubbling stream.

Beethoven's fame was spreading. On his daily walks, he strode briskly through Vienna's streets. When people spotted him, one person would whisper excitedly to another, "Beethoven!"

In 1809 Napoleon's troops again invaded Vienna. "Nothing but drums, cannons, and human misery in every form," Beethoven complained. "Curse this war!" Despite the noise, he wrote his Piano Concerto no. 5 in E-flat Major, the *Emperor* Concerto.

During this time, an important French diplomat visited Beethoven's apartment, where he lived alone. The man was shocked to see compositions all over furniture, bookshelves, and the floor. In one corner of the room stood a dust-covered piano with the lid raised and sheets of music scattered over the strings inside. Food-filled plates teetered on wooden chairs. Dirty clothes lay in heaps. Water splotches from Beethoven's many baths had stained the wood floor. Underneath Beethoven's piano was an unemptied chamber pot that he used as a toilet at night. Being neat wasn't important to Beethoven. Only music and the order of its notes mattered. Despite his anger about Napoleon's troops, Beethoven enjoyed his visitor and invited him to come back again.

Beethoven usually preferred old clothes to new ones. But in 1810, he fell in love with Therese Malfatti, his doctor's beautiful twenty-year-old niece. Suddenly, Beethoven ordered fashionable suits, fine cotton shirts, and silk neck scarves. He replaced his broken mirror so he could see his face. He wrote a piano piece for Therese called "Für Elise." But when he proposed marriage, Therese said no.

"He is an odd fellow," Therese's uncle said of Ludwig, "and perhaps the greatest of all geniuses."

In 1812 Ludwig's brother Johann married Therese Obermayer. The couple had lived together in Linz before their wedding. Ludwig didn't approve of either of his brothers' wives.

Though he had often been in love, Ludwig still hadn't found someone to marry. Feeling sad and lonely, Ludwig decided that he had to find happiness within himself, not from the outside world. But in July 1812, while staying at a health spa in Teplitz, Bohemia, he met Amalie Sebald, a singer from Berlin. She and Ludwig exchanged letters and may have been in love.

Another guest at the health spa was Johann Wolfgang von Goethe. Beethoven had admired him since his youth. A few months before, Beethoven had written music for one of Goethe's plays, a tragedy called *Egmont*. Beethoven's talent and energy impressed Goethe. But he thought the composer was difficult and stubborn—a rough, unsociable character with poor manners. Still, the two became friends.

One day in Teplitz when Goethe and Beethoven were on a walk, they met up with an empress. Goethe stepped aside to let her pass, removed his hat, and bowed low. Beethoven scowled and walked right on, barely tipping his hat. To him, royalty was in the mind, not in a title.

Although his hearing grew steadily worse, Beethoven gave several successful concerts the next year and completed more symphonies and shorter pieces.

"There is much to do on earth. Do it quickly!" read one of Beethoven's 1814 diary entries. Fascinated by all things mechanical, he used a metronome to mark time and wrote music for the panharmonicon, a huge mechanical organ that could make the sounds of many instruments. He even suggested the possibility of future inventions, such as fountain pens, elevators, and airplanes.

In 1814 Prince Karl Lichnowsky, fifty-eight, died. Beethoven had dedicated many of his works to this friend and supporter.

A year later, Ludwig's brother Carl, forty-one, died of tuberculosis on November 15, 1815. Carl's will made his wife Johanna and Ludwig both guardians of nine-year-old Karl. Over the next few years, Ludwig and Johanna fought over who would raise the child. Both Ludwig's music and health suffered as a result.

One bright spot during this troubling time happened in 1817. As other piano makers had before, an English company gave Beethoven a beautiful piano like no instrument he had ever played before. It had two pedals and spanned six octaves—all eight tones in a scale—more than other pianos of the time. Thrilled with the instrument's larger range, Beethoven immediately wrote music that made full use of its many keys and richer tones.

In 1818 Karl moved in with his uncle. Young Karl found his uncle's changing moods and unusual lifestyle difficult. Finally, in 1819, the courts gave Johanna custody of her son. Angry about the decision, Beethoven retreated into his work.

7

"Must It Be?"

Beethoven didn't stop trying to hear his music. He held a long, horn-shaped trumpet to his ear to make sounds louder. He rested his cheek on the piano to feel its thrumming beat. But he had become almost completely deaf. Beethoven had always been able to hear notes perfectly in his head. This was now his only way to test the sounds of different instruments blending as he composed.

Even if people shouted, he couldn't hear them. In 1819 people began writing to him in small booklets. Impatiently, Beethoven waited to read what people wrote. Then he answered out loud. These conversation books allowed him to discuss many topics—music, politics, and gossip. Beethoven always carried his conversation book, a sketchbook, and a thick pencil. He wore his spectacles on a chain around his neck so he wouldn't lose them.

By the time Beethoven turned fifty, he had withdrawn from all but a small group of relatives, close friends, and musicians. He no longer played the piano in public. Younger composers sometimes visited. Many of them—including Carl Maria von Weber, Gioacchino Rossini, and Franz Schubert—later became famous.

In 1822 he finished *Missa solemnis* ("solemn Mass" in Latin), a religious work for chorus and orchestra. Its blend of harmonies and notes was as colorful as a church's stained-glass windows. Beethoven seldom went to church or talked about his religious beliefs. But hints of his belief in God appeared in his letters, writings, and music.

In 1823 Beethoven, fifty-two, rented a house in Baden while working on his Ninth Symphony. He asked the landlord to put shutters on all the windows.

On the wood slats, he penciled his musical ideas and thoughts. These shutters became his diary, which he turned into six hundred pages of sketches. (The landlord later sold the shutters for gold.)

The first performance of Beethoven's Ninth Symphony took place in a crowded royal concert hall on May 7, 1824. Beethoven had insisted on conducting. Without his knowing it, the orchestra and chorus had been told to follow the main director, not Beethoven. Dressed in a formal black coat and breeches, white neckerchief, black silk stockings, and shoes with buckles, Beethoven had even tied back his wiry, graying hair. He lifted his arms high and waved them around, marking the beginning of each measure.

In the exciting last movement, a chorus sang a hymnlike poem, "Ode to Joy," that he had set to music. The symphony's final notes sounded in the hall.

"Bravo! Bravo!" the people shouted, stamping their feet. Beethoven remained bent over his printed music, his mouth turned down in a scowl. One of the soloists turned Beethoven around and pointed toward the audience. He saw people clapping, waving handkerchiefs, and smiling. Again and again, he bowed to applause he could not hear. The Ninth Symphony became one of Beethoven's most beloved works.

By this time, Beethoven's walks had become more rambling. Vienna's busy streets bustled with sounds. Horses' hooves clomped on the cobblestone streets. Vendors called out to sell their wares. People talked and laughed. But Beethoven's world had become completely silent.

He had moved so many times in his life that he often forgot his address. On one long walk, he got lost. Confused, tired, and hungry, he began peeking in the windows of houses. With ragged clothes and scraggly hair, he looked like a beggar. Someone reported him to the police, and they arrested him. Luckily, a local music director told the police who Beethoven was and gave him some clean clothes. The police sent him home.

As Beethoven's eyes grew weaker, he couldn't see to shave. He rarely brushed his teeth, except for nervously rubbing his front teeth with a napkin. Friends often secretly removed his tattered clothes and laid out new ones. Beethoven didn't even notice. He still enjoyed bathing and splashing in water, especially pouring water over himself. Sometimes water leaked to the floor below.

He slept and ate at odd times and complained about stomach pains. When doctors prescribed medicine, he gulped it all at once or forgot where it was. He tried a new cure for deafness—putting drops of milk filled with crushed nuts in his ears. It didn't help at all.

Little by little, Ludwig's relationship with his nephew had grown strained. He constantly asked Karl to help with music copying, talking to publishers, or shopping. Ludwig criticized some of Karl's friends. When he didn't visit often enough, his uncle scolded.

In early August 1826, nineteen-old Karl was unhappy with his uncle and depressed about university exams. Karl tried to end his life by shooting himself. The bullet only wounded him.

Afterward, Karl refused to see his uncle. When the two finally made up, Karl told Ludwig he wanted to join the army. Ludwig didn't object. For a change of scenery, they visited Ludwig's brother in late September. A wealthy pharmacist, Johann owned a country estate. There Karl could rest and heal.

Shortly after Ludwig arrived, he began composing outside in the crisp autumn air. Waving his arms as if conducting, he hummed, beat time with his hands and feet, and wrote in his notebook. Then he copied the parts for a new string quartet. On the fourth movement, he wrote "The Difficult Decision: Must it be? It must be, it must be! " No one was sure what Beethoven meant. The movement's slow, beginning notes seemed sad. Yet the ending was bright and happy.

In late November 1826, Ludwig and Karl set out for Vienna. On the way, Ludwig came down with chills and a fever that grew into pneumonia. Karl cared for his uncle before leaving for the army in January 1827. Bedridden, Ludwig's body swelled with fluid. Doctors operated to ease the pressure and pain. But Ludwig grew worse.

He wrote a letter to Franz Wegeler about their childhood friendship in Bonn: "I remember all the love you have always shown me." Beethoven said he still hoped to create more great works and then finish his life among kind people. He was pleased when a friend surprised him by sending the complete works of one of Beethoven's favorite composers, George Frideric Handel.

A loving circle of Ludwig's friends gathered around him. He told one visitor, "I shall, no doubt, soon be going above." Ludwig wrote a final will that left all of his possessions to his nephew Karl. Beethoven's strong body grew thin and weak. His eyes stayed closed most of the time. At last, he asked for a priest to give him a final blessing.

The morning of March 26, 1827, dawned cold and wintry. Late that afternoon, thunder boomed and lightning flashed. Beethoven opened his eyes briefly. Then he raised his clenched right fist in the air. A moment later, he was gone. After a while, friends lovingly snipped locks of his gray-streaked brown hair as keepsakes.

Word soon spread throughout Vienna that at fifty-six, the great Beethoven was dead. He had lived much longer than many people did at this time, but not long enough for those who loved him and his music.

The next day, his brother Johann and three of Ludwig's friends met to clean up his private papers and bundles of music. They also searched for bank shares that now belonged to Karl. Then they spotted a nail sticking out from a cabinet. When they pulled out the nail, a drawer came with it. It held the bank shares, some mementos, and something surprising. They found a passionate ten-page letter from Beethoven to a woman, written fifteen years before. In this letter, dated July 6, 1812, Beethoven had said, "My angel, my all, my very self. . . . My heart overflows with a longing to tell you so many things. . . . Be cheerful—and be for ever my faithful, my only sweetheart, my all, as I am yours."

No one knew who the woman in this letter was. But Beethoven had loved her deeply. Many call her his Immortal Beloved, the great love he longed for, but never had.

Afterword

On March 29, 1827, Beethoven's body lay in a flower-filled coffin, his head resting on a white silk pillow. Hour after hour, people filed solemnly past to see him once more. Then the coffin was closed. Musicians carried it along the streets leading to Trinity Church. Composers held torches high and walked on either side. A trombone choir played. Beethoven's brother Johann, nephew Karl, and his old friend Stephan von Breuning and Stephan's son Gerhard followed behind.

More than 20,000 people, including schoolchildren, joined the procession. Invited guests wore white silk scarves and lilies around their left sleeves, a sign of mourning. Inside the church, lighted candles glowed and musicians played Mozart's *Requiem*, a Mass for the dead. Two hundred horse-drawn carriages followed the elegant hearse to the gravesite. A friend and poet praised Beethoven as "among the great of all ages. . . . He was an artist, but a man, as well . . . in the highest sense. If he fled from the world, it was because in the depths of his loving nature he found no weapon against it. . . . He remained alone because he found no second Self [person to love]."

Etched on the simple headstone was one word: "Beethoven."

Ludwig van Beethoven was an extraordinary pianist. He was also one of the greatest composers of all time. Countless composers who lived after him studied his music. Bold ideas, remarkable energy, and simple melodies filled his best works. Beethoven once said that his music spoke from his heart to ours.

Fiercely interested in many forms of music, he wrote over 350 works—from pieces for small groups to soaring symphonies. Deafness slowly silenced his world, but not his music. Over 180 years after Beethoven's death, his music still rings across the ages.

Selected Works

Beethoven gave opus numbers to only 138 of his works, numbering over 350. Years listed are the years he finished the works.

1782 9 Variations in C Minor for piano on a march by Dressler
1783 3 Piano Sonatas (*Elector* Sonatas) in E-flat Major, F Minor, and D Major
1790 *Cantata on the Death of Emperor Joseph II*
1792 8 Variations in C on a theme by Count Waldstein for piano 4 hands
1796 12 Variations in G Major on Handel's "See the Conquering Hero Comes" from *Judas Maccabaeus* for cello and piano
1798 Violin Sonatas nos. 1–3 in D, A, and E-flat Major, op. 12
      Piano Sonata no. 8 in C Minor (*Pathétique*), op. 13
1800 Horn Sonata in F Major, op. 17
      Symphony no. 1 in C Major, op. 21
      5 Pieces for a mechanical clock
1801 Piano Sonata no. 14 in C-sharp Minor (*Moonlight* Sonata), op. 27/2
      The Creatures of Prometheus (ballet), op. 43
1802 Symphony no. 2 in D Major, op. 36
1804 Piano Sonata no. 21 in C Major (*Waldstein*), op. 53
      Symphony no. 3 in E-flat Major (*Eroica*), op. 55
      Christ on the Mount of Olives (oratorio), op. 85
1805 Piano Sonata no. 23 in F Minor (*Appassionata*), op. 57
      Fidelio (opera), op. 72
      Leonore Overture no. 2, op. 72b
1806 Symphony no. 4 in B-flat Major, op. 60
      Leonore Overture no. 3, op. 72c
1807 *Leonore* Overture no. 1, op. 138
1808 Symphony no. 5 in C Minor, op. 67
      Symphony no. 6 in F Major (*Pastoral*), op. 68
1809 Piano Concerto no. 5 in E-flat Major (*Emperor*), op. 73
      Piano Sonata no. 24 in F-sharp Major (also called "Für Therese"), op. 78
1810 *Egmont* Overture and Incidental Music, op. 84
      Bagatelle in A Minor for piano (also called "Für Elise")
1812 Symphony no. 7 in A Major, op. 92
      Symphony no. 8 in F Major, op. 93
1814 *Fidelio* (revised opera and overture), op. 72a
1815 *Calm Sea and Prosperous Voyage* (cantata), op. 112
1818 Piano Sonata no. 29 in B-flat Major (*Hammerklavier*), op. 106
1823 *Missa solemnis* in D Major, op. 123
1824 Symphony no. 9 in D Minor (*Choral*), op. 125
1826 String Quartet no. 16 in F Major, op. 135

Selected Bibliography

Quotes in the text are taken from sources marked by an asterisk (*).

*Beethoven, Ludwig van. *Beethoven: Letters, Journals and Conversations.* Translated and edited by Michael Hamburger. London: Thames and Hudson, 1951.

*Beethoven, Ludwig van. *The Letters of Beethoven.* 3 vols. Edited by Emily A. Anderson. New York: St. Martin's Press, 1961.

*Beethoven, Ludwig van. *Beethoven's Own Words.* Compiled by Philip Kruseman. London: Hinrichsen Edition Limited, 1947.

*Clive, Peter. *Beethoven and His World: A Biographical Dictionary.* New York: Oxford University Press, 2001.

*Cooper, Barry. *Beethoven.* New York: Oxford University Press, 2000.

Krull, Kathleen. *Lives of the Musicians: Good Times, Bad Times and What the Neighbors Thought.* San Diego: Harcourt Brace, 1993.

*Lockwood, Louis. *Beethoven: The Music and the Life.* New York: W. W. Norton, 2003.

*Marek, George. *Beethoven: Biography of a Genius.* New York: Crowell, 1969.

Martin, Russell. *Beethoven's Hair.* New York: Broadway Books, 2000.

Nichol, Barbara. *Beethoven Lives Upstairs.* New York: Orchard Books, 1993.

*Sonneck, O. J., ed. *Beethoven: Impressions of Contemporaries.* New York: G. Schirmer, 1926.

*Wegeler, Franz, and Ferdinand Reis. *Beethoven Remembered: The Biographical Notes of Franz Wegeler and Ferdinand Ries.* Arlington, VA: Great Ocean Publishers, 1987.

Websites about Ludwig van Beethoven

Beethoven the Immortal
http://www.lucare.com/immortal

Ira F. Brilliant Center for Beethoven Studies
http://www.sjsu.edu/depts/beethoven

Ludwig van Beethoven's Website
http://www.lvbeethoven.com/index_En.html

Mad about Beethoven
http://www.madaboutbeethoven.com

Index